NEHEMIAH
Courage in the Face of Opposition

12 studies
for individuals or groups

Don Fields

With Notes for Leaders

InterVarsity Press
Downers Grove, Illinois

InterVarsity Press
P.O. Box 1400
Downers Grove, IL 60515-1425
World Wide Web: www.ivpress.com

InterVarsity Press® *is the book-publishing division of InterVarsity Christian Fellowship/USA*®*, a student movement active on campus at hundreds of universities, colleges and schools of nursing in the United States of America, and a member movement of the International Fellowship of Evangelical Students. For information about local and regional activities, write Public Relations Dept., InterVarsity Christian Fellowship/USA, 6400 Schroeder Rd., P.O. Box 7895, Madison, WI 53707-7895, or visit the IVCF website at <www.ivcf.org>.*

Cover photograph: Andrew Wenzel/Masterfile

ISBN 0-8308-3033-2

Printed in the United States of America ∞

P	17	16	15	14	13	12	11	10	9	8	7	6	5	4	3	2	1
Y	16	15	14	13	12	11	10	09	08	07	06	05	04	03	02		

Contents

Getting the Most Out of *Nehemiah*

Nehemiah was in leadership during an extraordinary time in Israel's history. He faced opposition from all sides—both from his own people and from outside forces. A little background will help set the stage for understanding the pressures Nehemiah faced.

From antiquity, Ezra and Nehemiah have been considered almost as one book. The two books cover a period of about one hundred years. In 587 B.C. Judah was removed from the land of Israel and deported to Babylon with only a few left in the land. In 538 B.C. Cyrus sent some of the people back to rebuild the temple. Nehemiah's third return would be around 430 B.C. Zerubbabel, Ezra and Nehemiah are all wrapped up in this history. Zerubbabel built the temple, Ezra brought the law back into Israel's life, and Nehemiah rebuilt the wall that made Jerusalem secure.

The amazing thing is that Israel had more autonomy and distinctiveness during this period than at any time of their existence as a sovereign state. The Persian Empire allowed the people to practice their religious convictions with seriousness, and this probably accounts for why Israel had such a pristine religious life at this time.

Though Zerubbabel and Ezra worked more in the religious realm, Nehemiah was really sent to Judah to be governor of the land, and that gave him considerably more ability to make some lasting changes in the life of the people. The people needed Nehemiah's strong leadership to handle the opposition to their work.

There were three primary opposers: Sanballat, Geshem and Tobiah. Sanballat was probably governor of Samaria and was not interested in Judah becoming an independent nation again. Geshem is thought to have been a leader of a powerful block of Arab communities. Tobiah was probably governor of Ammon and a member of an influential Jewish family.

Derek Kidner describes the importance of this period of Israel's history:

> The two centuries of the Persian empire were among the most forma-
> tive periods of Jewish history. Out of the ruins of the little kingdom of
> Judah there had emerged the small community whose concern to be
> the people of God by pedigree and practice shaped it into the nation
> which meets us in the New Testament. Already the future prominence
> of the Temple and its priests, of the law and its scribes, as well as the
> enmity between Jew and Samaritans, could be seen developing.
> Throughout this time the Persian regime was given a substantial part
> to play, both in sending and subsidizing the three expeditions, of
> Zerubbabel, Ezra and Nehemiah, and in backing their authority with
> its own. It was not the first empire, nor the last, to be allotted some
> such role.*

The Israelites living in the land were fairly passive at this point in history. They had to adapt to the culture around them because they were such a small remnant. Their intermarrying and political ties made this considerably worse.

Nehemiah's gifts in administration and perseverance enabled him to mold this people back into the "people of God" so they could obey God's commands and have a distinction from the people around them. This is where Nehemiah shines through. It was not enough just to build the wall—he had to build a people that would once again stand on their own as God led them. Putting some "backbone" back into the people was a large part of what Nehemiah had to accomplish—even if it required him to be harsh with them at times.

God has called each of us to important tasks, both as leaders and as followers. Reading Nehemiah will help us to have the courage we need to follow through even in the face of difficulty and persecution. God be with you as you study Nehemiah.

Suggestions for Individual Study

1. As you begin each study, pray that God will speak to you through his Word.

2. Read the introduction to the study and respond to the personal reflection question or exercise. This is designed to help you focus on God and on the theme of the study.

3. Each study deals with a particular passage—so that you can delve into the author's meaning in that context. Read and reread the passage to be studied. The questions are written using the language of the New International Version, so you may wish to use that version of the Bible. The New Revised Standard Version is also recommended.

4. This is an inductive Bible study, designed to help you discover for yourself what Scripture is saying. The study includes three types of questions. *Observation* questions ask about the basic facts: who, what, when, where and how. *Interpretation* questions delve into the meaning of the passage. *Application* questions help you discover the implications of the text for growing in Christ. These three keys unlock the treasures of Scripture.

Write your answers to the questions in the spaces provided or in a personal journal. Writing can bring clarity and deeper understanding of yourself and of God's Word.

5. It might be good to have a Bible dictionary handy. Use it to look up any unfamiliar words, names or places.

6. Use the prayer suggestion to guide you in thanking God for what you have learned and to pray about the applications that have come to mind.

7. You may want to go on to the suggestion under "Now or Later," or you may want to use that idea for your next study.

Suggestions for Members of a Group Study

1. Come to the study prepared. Follow the suggestions for individual study mentioned above. You will find that careful preparation will greatly enrich your time spent in group discussion.

2. Be willing to participate in the discussion. The leader of your group will not be lecturing. Instead, he or she will be encouraging the members of the group to discuss what they have learned. The leader will be asking the questions that are found in this guide.

3. Stick to the topic being discussed. Your answers should be based on the verses which are the focus of the discussion and not on outside authorities such as commentaries or speakers. These studies focus on a particular passage of Scripture. Only rarely should you refer to other portions of the Bible. This allows for everyone to participate in in-depth study on equal ground.

4. Be sensitive to the other members of the group. Listen attentively when they describe what they have learned. You may be surprised by their insights! Each question assumes a variety of answers. Many questions do not have "right" answers, particularly questions that aim at meaning or application. Instead the questions push us to explore the passage more thoroughly.

When possible, link what you say to the comments of others. Also, be affirming whenever you can. This will encourage some of the more hesitant members of the group to participate.

5. Be careful not to dominate the discussion. We are sometimes so eager to express our thoughts that we leave too little opportunity for others to respond. By all means participate! But allow others to also.

6. Expect God to teach you through the passage being discussed and through the other members of the group. Pray that you will have an enjoyable and profitable time together, but also that as a result of the study you will find ways that you can take action individually and/or as a group.

7. Remember that anything said in the group is considered confidential and should not be discussed outside the group unless specific permission is given to do so.

8. If you are the group leader, you will find additional suggestions at the back of the guide.

---

*Derek Kidner, *Ezra & Nehemiah* (Downers Grove, Ill.: InterVarsity Press, 1971), p. 17

1

Depending on God

At one time or another, most of us have said, "I am too busy to pray!" If the work of God depended on our energy and insight, then it might be true. But of course, at least theoretically, we believe that God's work can only be done through his power. Psalm 127:1 says, "Unless the LORD builds the house, its builders labor in vain." Yet we don't think our biggest job is to pray.

GROUP DISCUSSION. How do you respond when you hear bad news about people you know and care for?

PERSONAL REFLECTION. How quickly do you identify with the problems of your friends?

As we go before the Lord in prayer we discover his perspective and gain confidence. Maybe that would make a difference in what we try to accomplish for the Lord. In this study Nehemiah models dependency on the Lord for his strength. *Read Nehemiah 1.*

1. In verses 1-3 what event is being discussed?

2. What four things does Nehemiah do when he hears Hanani's report?

3. List the specific concerns that Nehemiah mentions in his prayer (vv. 5-11).

4. How do you see the various elements of prayer being used here? (Consider the four parts of prayer: adoration, confession, thanksgiving and supplication.)

5. Are you using these forms of prayer in your prayer life? Why or why not?

6. What evidence do you find here that Nehemiah believed God heard his prayer and would answer it?

7. Nehemiah got more confident as he prayed and fasted. How did this prepare him to get more involved?

How does this compare with what you have experienced in prayer?

8. What do you learn about Nehemiah's character from his reaction and his prayer?

9. As you think about your ministry, are there any reports you are hearing that you need to petition God for?

10. What will you do to take a risk and become part of the answer for that prayer?

Pray for a situation you have heard about recently and have not gotten around to praying for yet.

Now or Later

For a two-week period, keep a list of concerns that people share with you. Take a few minutes at the end of your devotional time or before you go to bed to lift these concerns up to the Lord in prayer.

2

The Planning Process

Once, Dwight L. Moody was sailing on an ocean vessel and a fire broke out. One of his traveling companions said, "Don't you think we should go and pray, Brother Moody?" Moody replied, "You can go and pray, brother, but I am going to man the water buckets. There is a time to pray and a time to put the fire out!"

We tend to build a dichotomy between praying and doing—and in the end we neither pray nor do much. Usually what trips us up in the Christian life is failing to find the balance between dependency on God and action on our part. Surely both must be important in God's eyes!

GROUP DISCUSSION. Why do you think most Christians fail to do a "great work for God"? (For example, it might be because of lack of direction, feeling they lack giftedness, or simply laziness or apathy.) Explain.

PERSONAL REFLECTION. How do you feel when you think you are called to something, yet you are inexperienced in that area?

In this chapter Nehemiah shows evidence of careful planning on both fronts—praying and doing. *Read Nehemiah 2.*

---

1. How did Nehemiah give evidence of having a well-thought-through plan in verses 1-9?

2. What is the difference between the praying Nehemiah does in this chapter and what he did in chapter 1?

3. Would you have found it easy to take the risk Nehemiah took? Explain.

4. What evidences of thoroughness in planning do you find in verses 11-16?

5. Often people fall into one of two categories: (1) thorough planning or (2) going with the flow. Which do you usually follow and why?

6. Why do you think Nehemiah appears so confident in verses 17-20?

7. What do you see as the connection between Nehemiah's praying in chapter 1 and his confidence in chapter 2?

8. From these two chapters, what makes it reasonable for Nehemiah to be so hard-line with Sanballat, Tobiah and Geshem (vv. 18-20)?

9. When you do a great work for God, do you expect opposition? Explain.

10. Do you feel it is OK to say the "gracious hand of my God" is on the "good work" that you are doing (v. 18)? Explain why or why not.

11. Why is it important to enlist others in the body of Christ to do the work?

12. How can Nehemiah's example of praying, planning and boldness help you to take risks and action?

Pray for leaders in the body of Christ where you are, that they will get God's clear leading and be effective leaders.

Now or Later
Read Joshua 1, and meditate on leadership and the similarities between Joshua and Nehemiah. Think about why God could use these two men in leadership in Israel.

3

Working Together

Nehemiah 3

Many times leaders will have a great vision of what they think should be done, but they don't have commitment from the members of the group. A gifted leader can motivate others, but a job usually gets done because of prayer and unity among believers. This is so primarily because vision is spiritual and not material. When there is a lot of mundane work, like repairing a badly damaged wall, there must be unity for the job to be done. People need to feel they are part of the process or they won't usually commit to the work. To miss this step of getting people on board dooms most projects to failure!

GROUP DISCUSSION. What are your thoughts when you are part way into a job you thought others were committed to, only to find out you are one of the very few who are committed to the task?

PERSONAL REFLECTION. What motivates you to commit yourself to a group task that will take a lot of work?

This chapter describes the hard work of building the wall around Jerusalem and repairing the gates. *Read Nehemiah 3.*

---

1. Who are the major groups or individuals in this chapter who give themselves to the rebuilding work?

2. What part of the work would you feel motivated to do if you lived in Jerusalem?

3. What are some of the occupations of the repairers?

4. From the chapter, what seems to be the motivation for people to work on their part of the wall?

5. What does verse 5 tell us about the attitudes of some of the people in Jerusalem?

6. What was the place of women in this work (v. 12)?

7. What principles of division of labor do you see at work in this chapter?

How have you seen this principle applied in Christian circles?

8. Usually a natural progression in completing a project is (1) prayer, (2) vision, (3) strategy, (4) developing unity among the members and (5) doing the work. How have you seen this progression at work in any groups you have been part of?

_____

9. Does your church or fellowship group utilize many of your members in the work? Why or why not?

_____

10. How has cooperation played a significant part in your church or fellowship group's success in ministry?

_____

11. Do you feel you are as motivated to work in your church or fellowship as much as this group of people is? Explain your response.

Ask the Lord to give you a helper or partner in your ministry, and ask him to teach both of you how to work together.

Now or Later

During the week, observe in your church or fellowship group what percentage of the people do the work for the whole group. Evaluate why the percentages are what they are. Reflect on how you can be part of the solution.

4

Opposition from the Outside

Nehemiah 4

"Sticks and stones may break my bones, but names will never hurt me!" We usually hear children saying this. But when we want to oppose something because it is getting in our way, we adults have a slightly more sophisticated way of doing the same thing.

GROUP DISCUSSION. When have you seen a person or a group crumble under the pressure of opposition to the ministry?

PERSONAL REFLECTION. How have your plans for good and faithful service to the Lord been frustrated lately? Express your feelings to the Lord.

The enemies of Israel started out at the "sticks and stones" level, but they were soon into slander, intimidation and threatening with weapons. Our enemy the devil is always going to oppose the work of God. We need to expect and be able to fight opposition if we will do God's work. *Read Nehemiah 4.*

---

1. Describe the progression of seriousness in how Sanballat and Tobiah threaten the Jews and the building of the wall in verses 1-6.

2. What tends to be your response to concentrated opposition aimed at you and what you are doing?

3. How does Nehemiah respond to these forms of opposition (vv. 1-6)?

4. Why do you think Nehemiah is so uncharitable in his prayer in verses 4-5?

5. How do you think the attitude of the people in verse 6 affected the outcome of the work?

6. The enemies come up with many threats in verses 7-12. How many different kinds of threats do you find in these verses?

7. Note that Sanballat has inside help in his intimidation of the Jews and Nehemiah (vv. 10, 12). What is it, and what might be the circumstances that have caused these comments?

8. In verses 13-20, how does Nehemiah handle these threats?

9. In what situation have you seen a creative solution keep the work moving forward?

10. What was Nehemiah trusting in to get the work done (vv. 9, 14, 20)?

11. Does opposition make you want to quit a job, or does it challenge you to work harder to complete it? Explain.

12. What kinds of opposition does your Christian group and its leadership face?

13. How can you learn from Nehemiah's example in handling opposition?

Pray that God will give you strength to be creative in accomplishing your goals for him.

Now or Later

Think of an area of life where you have been bogged down or ineffective. Journal about how you can trust God for that area, and make a plan of action to overcome it. Share your plan with a good friend.

5

Opposition from Within

Nehemiah 5

Most organizations and nations fall apart because of opposition and deterioration from within. An idea is conceived, it gains adherence, people give themselves to it self-sacrificially, and it grows to fruition. Then, after it has served its purpose for a period of time, the work it took to get to that point is taken for granted, and often personal goals and desires corrupt the intended purpose. Usually someone figures out how to make money from the idea, and it is not long before that which helped people begins hurting people.

GROUP DISCUSSION. How do you react when people within your church or fellowship group fail to live out the character of your group's shared vision—when they start to use the group for personal reasons and not for the shared vision?

PERSONAL REFLECTION. How easily discouraged are you when people let you down? Explain.

In this chapter of Nehemiah we see self-sacrifice turn to self-interest. *Read Nehemiah 5.*

---

1. What three forms of internal opposition in verses 1-5 are developing against the vision of building the wall?

2. How would it affect your energy level to build a wall if you saw your daughter going into slavery for lack of money to pay the bills?

3. Who seem to be the people responsible for this inequity, and why do you think they would do this?

4. Make two columns. In the first cite the practices of the nobles, officials, former governors and their servants (vv. 7-12); in the second cite the practices of Nehemiah and his servants (vv. 14-18).

What comparisons and contrasts do you note?

5. How would you define the kind of leadership that Nehemiah exercises in dealing with this internal opposition to the wall?

6. In what ways are leaders (spiritual or secular) today likely to assume privileges as these nobles and officials did?

7. When have you seen a leader sacrifice a privilege to live according to God's values?

8. How do you determine what is culturally acceptable and what God's kingdom values are?

9. How well do you think Nehemiah did in fitting kingdom values and worldly values together?

10. In what ways does the chapter show Nehemiah doing all he can to not be part of this internal opposition?

11. What kind of internal opposition could likely come up within your church or Christian group to divert you from your real objectives, and how could you deal with that?

Think about opposition you are facing, and take it to the Lord for his answers. Pray that he will turn it for good.

Now or Later
Read through the book of Amos and make a list of the things God, through Amos, challenges the religious leaders to change in their lifestyle so they will care for people the way God does.

6

Facing Intimidation

Using power to create pressure is a very effective way to get at people, especially if they are not sure of themselves or what they are doing. However, if the objects of intimidation are quite confident in what they are doing, they may not be at all bothered by this approach. Nehemiah had wrestled with God so thoroughly about what he was doing in building the wall that he was not sidetracked by attempts to call him away from the work.

GROUP DISCUSSION. How do you react when people try to intimidate you regarding work you feel confident in doing?

How does your reaction differ if you are less confident about what you are doing?

PERSONAL REFLECTION. Think of a time when you had to fight for something you thought was right. How did you feel and act?

When someone reacts like Nehemiah, then the intimidator must become more and more threatening. It eventually boils down to who can intimidate the most, or who is the most confident in what God's will is for the occasion. Notice in this chapter that Nehemiah doesn't give in to the intimidation. *Read Nehemiah 6.*

---

1. What are some of the efforts at intimidation in this chapter?

---

2. If you had been Nehemiah, what would have been your reactions?

---

3. What kind of divided loyalties do you find in the people of this chapter?

---

4. What are some guiding principles Nehemiah gives about how to cooperate with other religious groups in your community or campus?

---

5. How is the work God has called you to do a "great work" and worthy of your full attention?

---

6. How could you make your vision for this "great work" more clear, so that you will not be easily sidetracked?

7. What do you expect by way of opposition in the job you are doing for the Lord?

8. What kind of potential sidetracks do you face?

9. How do the circumstances of verses 17-19 make keeping his objectives clear important for Nehemiah?

10. With this culture's emphasis on relationships and the desire not to rock the boat, how well do you think we face these problems within our Christian groups?

How could we face these problems better?

Pray that the religious communities you are involved with will be strengthened by God to keep perspective about the real job and not be sidetracked.

Now or Later

In a small group or a group of friends from your body of Christ, think through a recent difficulty faced by that group and how it should have been solved using Nehemiah's principles from this chapter.

7

Family History

I remember my grandparents talking about our family genealogy, and I thought, "How boring," so I didn't listen. Now I have six thousand names on my computer about my genealogy! I wish that I had listened to their conversations, because now I have lost much of the information with no way to retrieve it. I have even started recording many of my oldest relatives so that I get not only the information but also their voice on tape for future generations. ·

GROUP DISCUSSION. How many generations back can you go in tracing your family name?

PERSONAL REFLECTION. Recall a fond family memory that you have from a holiday or your childhood. Thank the Lord for giving you your past as a remembrance and guide for the future.

In this chapter of Nehemiah we find that if people could not trace their lineage back to a preexilic Jewish relative, they were not considered bona fide descendants and could not be counted. I wonder if some of them wish they had listened more to their relatives when they were talking about great grandpa and great grandma? *Read Nehemiah 7.*

---

1. In verses 1-3, what progress is Nehemiah making with his goals and objectives?

2. Are you proud or embarrassed about your family history? Explain.

3. What safeguards does Nehemiah take to protect Jerusalem?

4. We ran into Hanani before (1:2). From the qualifications given in verse 2, why could Nehemiah trust him?

5. Nehemiah decides that the families who have returned from exile should be registered. How would the registration force the people to deal with Israel's sin of mixing themselves with the people of the nations around them (vv. 63-65)?

6. Spiritual purity and practice were very low in Israel at this time, and most of these people had not lived on the family land for over a hundred years. What does Nehemiah's registration cause to happen here?

7. Why couldn't some of the people make connection with past relatives or their family inheritance?

Why would this be so important for religious leaders to be able to do?

8. In verse 73 many people settle in their towns. It is an agrarian society, and they make their living off of the land, which is their family inheritance. How difficult do you think it would be to populate Jerusalem if the main way you made your living was by farming?

_____

9. What does this tell you about why Nehemiah was concerned about safety in Jerusalem?

_____

10. In what ways are you concerned about your family history and protecting it?

_____

11. How far back can you identify Christians in your family and what they did for the Lord?

_____

12. How does the thought that you will be in someone's Christian family tree affect you?

Offer God a prayer of thanks for the good things you know about your family, and ask God to work in those people in your family who do not know him yet.

Now or Later

Go to the oldest people in your family and ask them about the people as far back as they can remember. Make up a family tree of your lineage and begin to write down some of the history of your family.

8

Revival

A look at Scripture and church history seems to indicate that mature Christians have a pretty wide variety of religious emotions. That is, they know how to laugh, and they know how to weep. Sometimes we avoid crying and laughing because it implies that we are not stable. When we deny a variety of religious emotions, we are robbing ourselves.

GROUP DISCUSSION. How much is celebration a part of your regular Christian life?

PERSONAL REFLECTION. People can sometimes be classified as either optimistic or pessimistic. Which do you feel best describes you?

This chapter of Nehemiah reveals real repentance, contrition and weeping, but also great celebration and joy in doing what God wants. Without the exhilaration of celebration our tears of repentance would lead us into morbid introspection—something that would do us no good, because only God can handle our sins and shortcomings. But without true repentance and contrition we really do not find joy of the kind this chapter demonstrates. *Read Nehemiah 8.*

---

1. The seventh month was one of great importance to the Jews. It was to include several feasts as well as the great Day of Atonement. How would you title this chapter given the theme of the chapter?

2. Because of what has happened in the previous chapter, what would prompt you to want to meet with all the other people who had built the wall?

———————————————————————————————

3. What were the qualifications of those who attended (vv. 2-3)?

———————————————————————————————

4. What statements show the reverence and seriousness of the people as they receive the Word of God (vv. 3-12)?

———————————————————————————————

5. How did the religious leaders help the people understand what the law was saying to them?

———————————————————————————————

6. In verses 9-12 Nehemiah and all the leaders try to encourage the people to celebrate after the revival and repentance they have gone through. Why do you think the people are weeping, and why do the religious leaders want them to celebrate?

———————————————————————————————

7. Why do you think God put so many feasts and celebration days in the Old Testament calendar?

———————————————————————————————

8. What is the counterpart to these celebrations in the church today?

———————————————————————————————

9. Compare your ability and willingness to celebrate with your show-ing repentance and contrition. Does one or the other come more easily? Explain.

10. Who assembles on the second day (v. 13), and why do you think they assemble?

11. In verses 12 and 17 it says that all the people had great joy. What was the reason for this?

12. How do Christians you know show the great joy they have from obeying God's Word?

13. Many Christians do not have much joy because they don't take obedience to God's Word seriously or make it a priority in their lives. How will you guard against that in your life?

Pray that God will give you a good balance between the heart attitude of contrition and repentance and the joy of celebrating God's forgiveness and grace toward you.

Now or Later
Talk to a good Christian friend about how they balance (1) sorrow and repentance for their sin and (2) celebrating what God has done for them. All Christians probably find this difficult at times, but both are important and have to be developed in the Christian life or we get unbalanced in our attitude toward God.

9

Confession
& Commitment

Nehemiah 9—10

Though we know we should and though we have every reason to do it, one of our greatest challenges is to own up to our sins and the sins of our family and really come clean before God.

GROUP DISCUSSION. Imagine you are the parent of a college graduate. You have tried to give them as good a start in life as you could, and now they are ready to launch out on their own. What do you expect of them in their relationship with you as their parent?

PERSONAL REFLECTION. How important is the confession of your wrong actions to you in your relationship with God?

The remnant of Israel knows they do not stand a chance to make it in Jerusalem without the help of God, so they are getting very honest with God and renewing their covenant with him. This is one of the more serious moments in Israel's history, before or after the exile. They are recognizing that everything they have belongs to God and they had better be good stewards of what he has given them. *Read Nehemiah 9—10.*

---

1. As you read Nehemiah 9, what stands out to you about Ezra's prayer?

2. What part does confession play in your Christian life?

3. Why do you think they spent so much time confessing and identifying with the sins of their ancestors?

4. Do you have any sense of history regarding the sins and shortcomings of your family? Explain your answer.

5. Thinking of family members who are still alive, do you intercede for them and their relationship with God? Why or why not?

6. Why do you think they had all the religious leaders sign the covenant?

7. In chapter 10, what groups of people are mentioned as covenant signers (vv. 1, 9, 14, 28, 34)?

8. As you look down through the chapter, list the things the Israelites are committing themselves to do.

9. In 10:29, what do we learn about the seriousness of this commitment they are making?

___

10. We often say that God is looking for character change in our lives. Why do you think this list of things falls so heavily on the material/physical side and not the spiritual?

___

11. In an agrarian society the current barter system would be more crops than coins. Why will the effectiveness of Jerusalem (wall, temple, economy and so on) have to depend on material as well as spiritual fidelity?

___

12. Explain how you work on the balance of the spiritual and the material/physical side of your Christian life.

Offer praise for people who encouraged you in the Lord and intercession for those who do not yet know the Lord and his life-changing power.

Now or Later

Journal for the next week about what you know of your family's spiritual journey and what this will teach you about your commitment to the Lord.

10

Big Decisions

When Ken is deciding where to live and work, he bases the decision on where he feels God wants him to develop a ministry and be of help in building up the body of Christ. Certainly people with the world's values do not choose a place to live and work on this basis. But as a Christian, the more I think about it, the more it makes sense. Not just my money belongs to the Lord but also my profession and gifts, so that they can be used in the body of Christ. God surely knows better than me where I should live and work so that I will fit his plans for the building of his kingdom! Only God can balance all the variables in a way that works best for his purposes.

GROUP DISCUSSION. What factors do you consider in determining where you live? (Consider occupation, salary, school, church, ministry, family and so on.)

PERSONAL REFLECTION. Does it seem strange to you that God is even interested in where you live?

Read Nehemiah 11.

1. How did the Jews in chapter 11 decide who would live in Jerusalem?

2. If it was decided by lot that you should live in Jerusalem, and you were a farmer with a piece of land fifteen miles from Jerusalem, how would you feel about the decision?

---

3. What reasons do you think the people might have to not want to live in Jerusalem?

---

4. What reasons can you think of for these five groups of people to live in Jerusalem (v. 3)?

---

5. List jobs or positions that would need to be filled in Jerusalem.

---

6. How (from chapter 10) would all of these people be taken care of materially?

---

7. How is the security and functioning of Jerusalem related to the Jews living in the towns around Jerusalem?

---

8. Would you rather be out in the fields producing crops or playing a supporting role in Jerusalem?

9. Since the land was given in perpetuity to the clan and family as an inheritance, what would have been the natural struggle of where to live?

10. Since our barter system is money, in what ways does our lifestyle free us up to be more involved in urban development and building the kingdom of God?

11. As you read this passage, what personal decisions (past and future) about where you live and how that impacts your service for God come to mind?

How does it help you clarify how you should make such decisions?

Pray to the Lord about decisions you have made in the past about where to live, and pray for guidance about any future decisions.

Now or Later

God's covenant with Israel in the Old Testament was very tied to a place. What differences do you perceive in the New Testament that makes it different for us as Christians than it was for the Old Testament Jews?

11

Service & Integrity

"If a job is worth doing, it is worth doing right!" I would like to have a dollar for every time I heard that growing up. I don't think that I understood the saying nearly as well as I do after years of working on it. Integrity and respect come to those who do a good job whatever they work at. We recognize excellence when we see it, and we are offended by a job half done. We would be of much better use to God, others and ourselves if we didn't volunteer for everything that comes along but rather did a better job on the things we can realistically complete. If I do my part faithfully, God will do the rest in building his kingdom.

GROUP DISCUSSION. Imagine a company's annual report recognizing the guard who walks around the company grounds between 11 p.m. and 7 a.m. That would be quite unusual. Why do you think we see some jobs as important and others as menial?

PERSONAL REFLECTION. What jobs do you do that give you a lot of fulfillment and satisfaction?

Read Nehemiah 12.

1. Why do you think the author mentions so many people in this chapter?

2. How do you generally appreciate the support roles of the people in your church or fellowship group?

3. How would you feel if you were Meshullam in verse 25 and were recognized for guarding the storerooms?

4. Consider verses 8 and 24. Do you think most people would have wanted these jobs? Why or why not?

5. Since in our culture we see the up-front gifts as more significant than the supporting or helping gifts, would you see being in the choir as an important ministry? Explain.

6. Notice verse 43. From what you have read in Nehemiah so far, what is the reason for this great rejoicing?

7. How do you think all the people of Israel felt at this celebration, and how did the people around Israel feel when they heard the rejoicing?

8. How do you and the body of Christ around you feel when you have completed a job that everyone has been involved in?

---

9. Look at verses 44-47. How important do you think the collection of these goods was to the effective running of Jerusalem and providing the worship and celebration that Jerusalem represented?

---

10. How are the supporting roles in your church or fellowship valued and recognized?

---

11. How could you give (financially and with your encouragement) to sustain the supporting people (that is, church secretaries, missionaries of all sorts, youth workers, various workers at denominational headquarters and so on) in your church or fellowship life?

Pray that you will find true satisfaction in your work for the body of Christ.

Now or Later
Go to the leadership in your church or fellowship and ask what job you can do to help your group function better.

12

Love That Challenges

"I know they are sinning against the Lord, but I love them too much to reprimand them."

Sometimes we emphasize loving people and not endangering our relationship with them over challenging them to get right with the Lord. When we think like this, we have accepted the world's values and not kingdom values. If relationship with God is the most important thing in the world, then to help people get back into right relationship with God is the best thing we can do for them. When we don't do this, what we are really saying is that we are more concerned about what that person thinks than what God thinks.

GROUP DISCUSSION. Why do you think we find it so hard in this culture to correct a brother or a sister in the Lord?

PERSONAL REFLECTION. We all make promises to God that we sometimes fail to keep. How do you handle it when you sin again?

Note from 2:1 and 13:6 that Nehemiah spent twelve years in Jerusalem before going back to Artaxerxes. We don't know how long it was before Nehemiah came back to Jerusalem to check up on things, but it was probably several years. Chapter 13 tells us how things stood on his return. *Read Nehemiah 13.*

---

1. What are the indications in this chapter that the Israelites have backslidden before the Lord?

---

2. What happened when someone came to you to correct you or you went to someone to correct them?

---

3. Considering the people made such a strong covenant in chapter 10, how do you think they could have gone this far astray in chapter 13?

---

4. What does the passage reveal about how Nehemiah felt when he came back and saw how bad things were spiritually?

---

5. Compare 10:30 with 13:23-28. Do you see anything in the text that shows you why Israel has backslidden?

---

6. Why is it so much harder to confront leaders who are sinning than regular pew-sitting church members?

7. What right does Nehemiah have to be so harsh on people in verse 25?

8. Nehemiah's response in verse 25 is very dramatic and physical. What principles does this suggest to you for how we should deal with sin today?

9. Why does Nehemiah take such drastic action in verses 6-7 and verse 28?

10. In what ways do you need to be more direct with others about their sin?

11. How would you like others to help you in dealing with your own sin?

Pray that in the body of believers we will not let people wander into sin and out of fellowship with God and with other Christians.

Now or Later
Ask three or four friends in your fellowship group to join in an accountability group, and encourage one another to serious, consistent Christian living. Use Matthew 18:15-22 as a resource.

Leader's Notes

MY GRACE IS SUFFICIENT FOR YOU. (2 COR 12:9)

Leading a Bible discussion can be an enjoyable and rewarding experience. But it can also be *scary*—especially if you've never done it before. If this is your feeling, you're in good company. When God asked Moses to lead the Israelites out of Egypt, he replied, "O Lord, please send someone else to do it"! (Ex 4:13). It was the same with Solomon, Jeremiah and Timothy, but God helped these people in spite of their weaknesses, and he will help you as well.

You don't need to be an expert on the Bible or a trained teacher to lead a Bible discussion. The idea behind these inductive studies is that the leader guides group members to discover for themselves what the Bible has to say. This method of learning will allow group members to remember much more of what is said than a lecture would.

These studies are designed to be led easily. As a matter of fact, the flow of questions through the passage from observation to interpretation to application is so natural that you may feel that the studies lead themselves. This study guide is also flexible. You can use it with a variety of groups—student, professional, neighborhood or church groups. Each study takes forty-five to sixty minutes in a group setting.

There are some important facts to know about group dynamics and encouraging discussion. The suggestions listed below should enable you to effectively and enjoyably fulfill your role as leader.

Preparing for the Study

1. Ask God to help you understand and apply the passage in your own life. Unless this happens, you will not be prepared to lead others. Pray too for the various members of the group. Ask God to open your hearts to the message of his Word and motivate you to action.

2. Read the introduction to the entire guide to get an overview of the

entire book and the issues which will be explored.

3. As you begin each study, read and reread the assigned Bible passage to familiarize yourself with it.

4. This study guide is based on the New International Version of the Bible. It will help you and the group if you use this translation as the basis for your study and discussion.

5. Carefully work through each question in the study. Spend time in meditation and reflection as you consider how to respond.

6. Write your thoughts and responses in the space provided in the study guide. This will help you to express your understanding of the passage clearly.

7. It might help to have a Bible dictionary handy. Use it to look up any unfamiliar words, names or places. (For additional help on how to study a passage, see chapter five of *Leading Bible Discussions,* InterVarsity Press.)

8. Consider how you can apply the Scripture to your life. Remember that the group will follow your lead in responding to the studies. They will not go any deeper than you do.

9. Once you have finished your own study of the passage, familiarize yourself with the leader's notes for the study you are leading. These are designed to help you in several ways. First, they tell you the purpose the study guide author had in mind when writing the study. Take time to think through how the study questions work together to accomplish that purpose. Second, the notes provide you with additional background information or suggestions on group dynamics for various questions. This information can be useful when people have difficulty understanding or answering a question. Third, the leader's notes can alert you to potential problems you may encounter during the study.

10. If you wish to remind yourself of anything mentioned in the leader's notes, make a note to yourself below that question in the study.

Leading the Study

1. Begin the study on time. Open with prayer, asking God to help the group to understand and apply the passage.

2. Be sure that everyone in your group has a study guide. Encourage the group to prepare beforehand for each discussion by reading the introduction to the guide and by working through the questions in the study.

3. At the beginning of your first time together, explain that these studies are meant to be discussions, not lectures. Encourage the members of the group to participate. However, do not put pressure on those who may be hes-

itant to speak during the first few sessions. You may want to suggest the following guidelines to your group.

☐ Stick to the topic being discussed.

☐ Your responses should be based on the verses which are the focus of the discussion and not on outside authorities such as commentaries or speakers.

☐ These studies focus on a particular passage of Scripture. Only rarely should you refer to other portions of the Bible. This allows for everyone to participate in in-depth study on equal ground.

☐ Anything said in the group is considered confidential and will not be discussed outside the group unless specific permission is given to do so.

☐ We will listen attentively to each other and provide time for each person present to talk.

☐ We will pray for each other.

4. Have a group member read the introduction at the beginning of the discussion.

5. Every session begins with a group discussion question. The question or activity is meant to be used before the passage is read. The question introduces the theme of the study and encourages group members to begin to open up. Encourage as many members as possible to participate, and be ready to get the discussion going with your own response.

This section is designed to reveal where our thoughts or feelings need to be transformed by Scripture. That is why it is especially important not to read the passage before the discussion question is asked. The passage will tend to color the honest reactions people would otherwise give because they are, of course, supposed to think the way the Bible does.

You may want to supplement the group discussion question with an icebreaker to help people to get comfortable. See the community section of *Small Group Idea Book* for more ideas.

You also might want to use the personal reflection question with your group. Either allow a time of silence for people to respond individually or discuss it together.

6. Have a group member (or members if the passage is long) read aloud the passage to be studied. Then give people several minutes to read the passage again silently so that they can take it all in.

7. Question 1 will generally be an overview question designed to briefly survey the passage. Encourage the group to look at the whole passage, but try to avoid getting sidetracked by questions or issues that will be addressed later in the study.

8. As you ask the questions, keep in mind that they are designed to be used just as they are written. You may simply read them aloud. Or you may prefer to express them in your own words.

There may be times when it is appropriate to deviate from the study guide. For example, a question may have already been answered. If so, move on to the next question. Or someone may raise an important question not covered in the guide. Take time to discuss it, but try to keep the group from going off on tangents.

9. Avoid answering your own questions. If necessary, repeat or rephrase them until they are clearly understood. Or point out something you read in the leader's notes to clarify the context or meaning. An eager group quickly becomes passive and silent if they think the leader will do most of the talking.

10. Don't be afraid of silence. People may need time to think about the question before formulating their answers.

11. Don't be content with just one answer. Ask, "What do the rest of you think?" or "Anything else?" until several people have given answers to the question.

12. Acknowledge all contributions. Try to be affirming whenever possible. Never reject an answer. If it is clearly off-base, ask, "Which verse led you to that conclusion?" or again, "What do the rest of you think?"

13. Don't expect every answer to be addressed to you, even though this will probably happen at first. As group members become more at ease, they will begin to truly interact with each other. This is one sign of healthy discussion.

14. Don't be afraid of controversy. It can be very stimulating. If you don't resolve an issue completely, don't be frustrated. Move on and keep it in mind for later. A subsequent study may solve the problem.

15. Periodically summarize what the group has said about the passage. This helps to draw together the various ideas mentioned and gives continuity to the study. But don't preach.

16. At the end of the Bible discussion you may want to allow group members a time of quiet to work on an idea under "Now or Later." Then discuss what you experienced. Or you may want to encourage group members to work on these ideas between meetings. Give an opportunity during the session for people to talk about what they are learning.

17. Conclude your time together with conversational prayer, adapting the prayer suggestion at the end of the study to your group. Ask for God's help in following through on the commitments you've made.

18. End on time.

Many more suggestions and helps are found in *Leading Bible Discussions,* which is part of the LifeGuide Bible Study series.

Components of Small Groups

A healthy small group should do more than study the Bible. There are four components to consider as you structure your time together.

Nurture. Small groups help us to grow in our knowledge and love of God. Bible study is the key to making this happen and is the foundation of your small group.

Community. Small groups are a great place to develop deep friendships with other Christians. Allow time for informal interaction before and after each study. Plan activities and games that will help you get to know each other. Spend time having fun together—going on a picnic or cooking dinner together.

Worship and prayer. Your study will be enhanced by spending time praising God together in prayer or song. Pray for each other's needs—and keep track of how God is answering prayer in your group. Ask God to help you to apply what you are learning in your study.

Outreach. Reaching out to others can be a practical way of applying what you are learning, and it will keep your group from becoming self-focused. Host a series of evangelistic discussions for your friends or neighbors. Clean up the yard of an elderly friend. Serve at a soup kitchen together, or spend a day working on a Habitat house.

Many more suggestions and helps in each of these areas are found in *Small Group Idea Book.* Information on building a small group can be found in *Small Group Leaders' Handbook* and *The Big Book on Small Groups* (both from Inter-Varsity Press). Reading through one of these books would be worth your time.

Study 1. Nehemiah 1. Depending on God.

Purpose: To show that without prayer we probably won't risk great things for God. Nehemiah's confidence grows as he prays!

Question 1. This is not just theoretical to Nehemiah. He deeply cares about Jerusalem and how the people are getting along. And without a wall, he is pretty sure how they are getting along!

Question 2. It was customary among Jewish people to do these spiritual exercises. Even in Israel today, there is the wailing wall, and it is used regularly. Weeping, fasting and praying show our earnestness toward God. They show just how dependent we are on him. This is why they were in exile. He knows he must be serious with God.

Question 3. Nehemiah is concerned about the people's relationship with God, about confessing their sins and about God's promise to Israel to gather them back into the land. He prays for help from the king. Nehemiah knows they are in exile because they have not responded properly to God in the past.

Question 6. Nehemiah assumes God hears him and will answer his prayers. He is confident in God's ability, so he asks boldly. He is familiar with history and knows God's faithfulness to Israel in the past. He seems to trust God explicitly for his safety and the welfare of Israel.

Question 7. The point is that Nehemiah thinks about what his needs are and believes God will act for him. We find it hard to wed holy piety and the hard work of planning. We somehow think that God will come through irrespective of what we do. That is not a biblical pattern. God will do his part, but only if we will do our part! This is an issue of faith. I believe God can do it, or he cannot!

Question 9. When we hear of ministry needs and concerns, we need to commit ourselves to pray for these and to be ready to be part of God's answer to get the work done.

To summarize: as a cupbearer, Nehemiah is a man of high position in Susa. The cupbearer was often the right-hand man to the king and the financial controller in the country. He was a man of great influence but also a man who had big thoughts about God and could trust God for big things for himself and Israel. Jerusalem had been destroyed by Nebuchadnezzer II 140 years before this time. There was no security or safety for the people in Israel, and Nehemiah recognizes this as a very important issue if Israel was to become a stable and viable people before God and the surrounding nations.

Study 2. Nehemiah 2. The Planning Process.
Purpose: To see how Nehemiah takes a risk in his planning.
Group discussion. Any of these may be possible reasons, but I think that laziness and apathy are the major reasons most people don't attempt great things for God.

Question 1. He seems to know just what to ask from the king. He needs to be prepared because he doesn't seem to go before the king frequently. It was not uncommon in the ancient world to have many cupbearers, and they might not go before the king except occasionally when their turn came around. They might only serve a couple of months out of the year.

Question 2. It was long and protracted in chapter 1. Here it is very brief and done probably while he is doing other things.

Question 3. The risk is probably having a sad countenance. In ancient cultures you could be executed for bringing anything negative before a king. Nehemiah was taking a great risk, but he was convinced about what God wanted him to do.

Question 4. If Nehemiah only gets one time before the king, he knows what he will need. It basically unfolds in time, just like he asked the king!

Question 5. People feel strongly about both of these reactions. In a group of six to eight people, you will probably have both styles represented. Help them see both ways are neither right nor wrong, but they will have to be well thought through.

Question 6. Nehemiah's confidence is not in his abilities but comes from prayer. He may also know how frustrated the Jews are about their vulnerability and protection for their families.

Question 8. It is not so obvious to us, but it seems these three men were not really working for Israel's good. They gained their notoriety at the expense of Israel. We must also remember that they were not Jewish, and they had been the leaders in this land for a long time.

Question 9. Most people in the Bible faced opposition in their work. In our culture we feel like opposition must mean we are not in God's will. We cannot expect the evil one to let us build the kingdom of God without challenge. He will always try to thwart the work of God.

Study 3. Nehemiah 3. Working Together.

Purpose: To show that we must involve a good number of our group in the vision or else many jobs are not going to be done.

Question 1. Think here about priests, leaders, rulers, women, families and so on.

Question 2. Thinking about Jerusalem in the time of Nehemiah, what would you feel you could help with in this project? In your church or fellowship group, what would you like to do for the good of the whole group?

Question 3. Note that there is a great division of labor here. It seems as if everyone is working. It is a good feeling when all your friends are committed to the task.

Question 4. Nehemiah counted on natural motivation when he had people work on the part of the wall that was near their homes. They would want that part of the wall or gate to be well built and secure.

Question 5. If we don't anticipate opposition to our task, we can be blown away when that opposition occurs. No jobs are accomplished because one hundred percent of the people are committed to the job. Human nature does not seem to allow it to be that way.

Question 6. The casual reference to the daughters helping in verse 12 seems to imply that it was natural for women to be working alongside men. In an agrarian society, women often worked with the men.

Question 7. People probably worked on a section near their homes and businesses because they felt responsible for that area. Priests worked together because they lived near each other. Natural groupings seemed to form out of common interests. Jerusalem was broken down into sections where people of the same trade worked and lived.

Question 8. These elements can be seen in what we have read so far: prayer and vision in Nehemiah 1, strategy in Nehemiah 2:13-16, unity in Nehemiah 2:17-18 and the work in Nehemiah 3.

Question 9. Usually 20 percent of the Christians do 80 percent of the work in any group. Often the 20 percent complain of burnout. However, one of the hallmarks of growing, effective groups is that more than 20 percent of the people do the work. If too few people are in on the making of the vision statement for the group, you can be sure that it will be a struggle to keep people committed to the vision and the work.

Now or later. Reasons might be laziness, apathy, commitment, delegation, cliquishness and so on.

Study 4. Nehemiah 4. Opposition from the Outside.

Purpose. To show that as each difficulty comes, we must face it head-on and persevere for God and trust him for what we need to finish the job.

Question 1. The enemies start with what seems silly and petty ridicule, but it soon gets much more serious, to the point of threatening the army of Samaria.

Question 3. Nehemiah deals with the threats rather than ignoring them. He prays after most every threatening situation.

Question 4. They are not just making fun at the Jews expense; they would kill them if there was a good way to justify it to the Persians. This is a life-and-death situation.

Question 5. With all the intimidation going on, it is amazing that the people were so unified that they worked "with all their heart." They were surely motivated by a strong desire to see the wall built. They also wanted protection for themselves and their families.

Question 6. Some of the Jews were scared by the threats and were buckling under the pressure. Frustration is expressed by some of the Jews (probably those with allegiance to the enemies) living inside Jerusalem.

Question 7. Remember that the Jews have been under their Samaritan leadership for many years. There has been intermarriage and many other alliances with the people of the land. Nehemiah is up against a divided constituency, trying to unify them to be the people of God.

Question 8. He posts guards. He gives them all a challenging pep talk. He divides his work force into half working and half guarding the others. He works out a strategy and plan, and everyone returns to the work.

Question 9. There will be opposition to every plan, and you have to believe that God will help you do the work and move forward.

Question 11. Nehemiah is a man of great faith and great action. He knows God must bless their efforts, but he also knows they have to build the wall. He brings faith and action together into a dynamic plan and does not give in to the intimidation.

Questions 12-14. We often function as though opposition must mean that God doesn't want us to keep doing the job, when the opposite is true. God wants us to grow in faith and trust him in the face of opposition. Maybe you can do evangelism, not by the door-to-door approach, but you could have investigative Bible studies in homes or rooms and accomplish the same purpose. Be creative in finding new ways to face opposition and take risks.

Study 5. Nehemiah 5. Opposition from Within.

Purpose: To show how human nature moves people to better their own situation at the expense of others. True leadership is characterized by sacrifice and servanthood.

Question 1. It is often true that when leadership is like this the demise of a group occurs rather rapidly. Remember there were many years of no spiritual leadership and people were looking out for themselves.

Question 2. It is hard to throw yourself into the vision when terrible things are happening to your family, children, property and so on.

Question 3. The Jews were used to seeing the governor and his assistants set apart from the common people, and this may be why people did not recognize what the leaders were doing for a while. We tend to imitate what we see.

Question 4. When you make this list it becomes evident how much of a servant Nehemiah is and how self serving the others have been. Note from the chapter just how difficult it is for people to argue against Nehemiah's lifestyle! Sometimes when the contrast is so stark, arguing the point doesn't do much good.

Question 5. Nehemiah is a strong leader, but he is also a sacrificial and serving person. His lifestyle is clearly characterized by serving. Nehemiah is not bashful about pointing out his own integrity.

Questions 6-7. Human nature seeks to gain the advantage over people. When there is a limited amount of natural resources, the world will think it is ingenious and clever to gain as much of those natural resources as it can, even at the expense of others. Obviously God saw this problem and made the land in Israel always available to each family—even if it had to return to them in the year of Jubilee (every fifty years, Lev 25). The answer here is to return the land and the children to their original owners. Communism used this idea but was soon corrupted by the evil in human hearts. (This also occurs in societies in which the government is capitalistic, socialistic, monarchic, dictatorial or any other form.) The problem is not government but the human heart. Christians must deal with this; it isn't that there is a scarcity of all that is needed by people, because God is the supplier. But by the same token, God expects Christians to sacrifice and share what they have with others. God determines the flow of natural resources, not our cleverness or ingenuity.

Question 8. Kingdom values recognize the good of others in the body. These practices could not have been in line with God's will. Nehemiah's actions are recognizable as godly.

Question 9. We do not know for sure, but the integrity of Nehemiah shows he is fast using up his wealth for the good of Israel. There is a great outlay of wealth happening here, both in food and in buying back Israelite slaves.

Question 10. We can do Christian things for a lot of the wrong motives: (1) people make me look good; (2) I will upgrade my circle of friends and influences; (3) I will gain prestige, power or popularity and so on.

Study 6. Nehemiah 6. Facing Intimidation.

Purpose: To show how the leader reacts to the inevitable opposition that comes when we do the work of God.

Group discussion. Many times when people are intimidated they will get discouraged that things are not going as smoothly as they hoped, and they lose heart in the project. People are easily discouraged from the completion of many tasks.

Question 1. From conferences to threats of reports to the king to internal politics of marriage and loyalty oaths, the enemy is trying to do everything they can to stop the work. Persistent opposition grates on our nerves and robs us of our confidence, but the true leader keeps the perspective.

Question 2. We often react rather than act. The issues are intensified because we make it an us-them situation and only produce more arguing. Nehemiah sticks to stating his purpose and not arguing.

Question 3. In the ancient world families stayed close together, and it provided a certain amount of protection. Intermarrying tied people into a larger network of family structures and thus provided more protection. It was specially the nobles who had intermarried with the enemies of Israel (probably before Nehemiah came on the scene), likely in an attempt to gain a certain security from the non-Jewish nobles of the land. This produced formidable opposition to Nehemiah's building loyalty among the Jews already in Jerusalem.

Question 4. Opposition often comes from other religious people around where we live and work. The people of the land who married Jews probably took on the religion of the Jews as well. Nehemiah had a sense of keeping the religion of Israel more pure. Later, if you could not trace your lineage back to a preexilic family, you could not be counted as a true Jew. The nobles of Israel were not as desirous of that purity as Nehemiah was. Later Nehemiah brought them to a point where all foreign wives (or husbands) were turned loose for the sake of purity of religious convictions. If a religious group is not clear on the authority of the Scriptures or the person and work of Jesus Christ, we cannot agree with them and be in total fellowship. God sets guidelines of what is right and wrong, and we obey and trust him for the outcome.

Question 5. In the immediate context the Israelites are building the wall and their enemies are hindering it. When a ministry is God's, we should serve with all our hearts. Even though I may not see the larger picture of which my work is only a part, I should do it heartily for the Lord and trust him that all the pieces will fit together.

Questions 6-7. In biblical culture, people were more used to conflict and opposition. In our culture we interpret conflict and opposition as meaning God must not want us to continue the job. We do not know how to handle conflict, so we avoid it. Any good leader should realize that if it is God's work, then it will be opposed by someone, because the devil won't sit while God accomplishes his work.

Question 8. The group needs to think seriously how their divided loyalties to God and their network of friends can rob them of really being on God's side unconditionally. Christians are often robbed of experiencing reality with God because they are trying hard to serve God and man. Reality doesn't exist with equal parts God and the world. It lies in being sold out for God and not letting the things of this world become such high priorities.

Question 9. Satan doesn't want things to be easy; he makes them complicated fast. There is duplicity on the part of the nobles in Jerusalem because of politics and family relationships, so there is plenty to make things complicated. Satan knows this will make it difficult for Nehemiah and his concern for purity of the people of God.

Study 7. Nehemiah 7. Family History.

Purpose: To see that we are not in the family we are in by chance. God is sovereign and has placed us where he wants us to be for his glory and the building of his kingdom.

Group discussion. Some people in your group will know a lot about their family, and others will know almost nothing because of divorce and bad feelings in the family.

Question 1. Things are shaping up fast to give the people of Israel a safe place to be, where they will not be overly hassled by the people around them.

Question 2. Be aware that some people will be very embarrassed about their family and maybe even not want to talk about them. Others could talk you to death about their family. Be ready for both of these reactions and try not to make too strong of value judgments about either side.

Question 3. Not only are the walls and gates in place to secure Jerusalem, but now Nehemiah is working on having all the people take responsibility in their homes and neighborhoods. Jerusalem has not been functioning as a governing city for a long time, and now it is going to be governed and function well.

Question 4. When we consider all the divided loyalties the nobles of Israel had with the surrounding people of the land, it is very important to look at who Nehemiah puts in charge. From beginning to end, Nehemiah's number one problem is getting the people of Israel back into a strong relationship with God as his covenant people. The Israelites want to mix God and the world together.

Question 5-7. The whole purpose of the wall was to make Israel into a self-sustaining nation again under God. Safety, having their own land, marriage and thus family purity are all important for Israel to be the covenant people again that God wants them to be. Note that if people know who the "true Jews" are, then all the surrounding nationalities who are trying to be part of Israel will be seen for what they are—foreigners! Study verses 61-65, and think about the effects of this registration for outsiders. The law specifically stipulated that the land had to return to its original owner every fifty years. The only way you could own land in Israel was if you could trace your lineage back to the original Jewish inheritors of the land. This is one of the means that Nehemiah uses to maintain national and religious purity as God's people.

Question 8. Jerusalem meant safety, but they farmed the land outside the walls of Jerusalem. All these people who were priests, Levites, temple attendants, singers and so on used to get their living by the offerings brought to the temple. Those offerings were slim, and they wanted to farm their land to make ends meet. They would be taking a chance by living in Jerusalem and depending on offerings for their livelihood.

Questions 10-12. Our family heritage should help us learn and grow from our ancestors' mistakes or successes. To not pay attention to family history is to repeat it. Many times we react to our families rather than working through those relationships. When we do this, we usually don't learn very much. Since Israel was judged by God and sent into captivity, the people who came back from Babylon might have wanted to forget their relatives. In doing so, they might also have fallen into the same traps their families fell into that brought judgment on them. Throughout Scripture this forgetting is a sin that God often challenges. All of us will find that we have some good memories from our families as well as bad memories.

Study 8. Nehemiah 8. Revival.

Purpose: To show the need for God's Word to bring revival to our hearts. God's Word also brings celebration to us as the hope of God's forgiveness, mercy and response to our repentance and contrition. This is epitomized by the Day of Atonement.

Question 1. After the hard work of building the wall and securing their safety from their enemies around them, it is time to get their spiritual lives in tune. The law, the proper response to the law and renewal of the covenant with God are the first order. A title might be "Patching Things Up with God."

Questions 2-3. It is natural to rejoice when you have accomplished something that most people would say was impossible, especially when both you and your enemies are aware of the hand of God in the accomplishing of the task. They know why they were sent into exile and that God was faithful to bring them out again. It would be natural to not want to repeat the mistakes of the past. They want to know this God who has worked in their favor and they are serious about trying to understand what he wants. Everyone who has reached the age of reasoning feels the need to understand more about this.

Question 4. Statements that show the seriousness are (1) they stood at the reading of the Word, (2) they lifted their hands and said amen, (3) they bowed down and worshiped the Lord with their faces toward the ground, and (4) they wept when they understood the Word. It is obvious that their hearts were prepared by repentance and contrition so that the Word was having its effect on their lives. All of these actions were common in the culture of that time, especially before kings, emperors and rulers. This is reverence.

Question 5. Remember, at this time not many of the people of captivity would read the law on their own, and since the language of the area is Aramaic they might need translation. Most are not familiar with the law of God as it has not been operating for quite some time. As adults this might be the first time they have ever understood it.

Questions 6-7. It is important that they repent and are contrite. But the Day of Atonement is the number one time of the year that also shows the hope they have in God, and it is time to celebrate! Had their tears happened at a non-feast time, the religious leaders would not have been so bent on getting them to celebrate. Can you imagine Easter happening during a week of national mourning and repentance? The repentance is important, but the celebration is also a great reminder of what God offers us in repentance.

Question 8. Worship and the Lord's Supper certainly come to mind.

Question 9. In our culture we tend to not take sin, contrition and repentance very seriously. But true life with God starts there! Now we need to balance that with the hope of forgiveness and heaven, which should make us want to celebrate.

Question 10. The religious leaders of Israel are responsible to God to lead the people and set the pace for them in seeking and obeying God. People need leaders. When leaders don't lead according to God's ways, it is downhill for everybody.

Question 11-13. Probably the most important point of this chapter is that when we obey God's Word, it will produce great joy in our hearts. God wants us to know that joy, but it is not known apart from contrition and confession. Apparently Israel had not known that joy for quite some time, and it was exhilarating.

It is important that the people in your group see this connection between joy and obedience. Get them talking about how this works out in their lives. Is it an experience that they are familiar with? Be ready to talk about confession and how people can do that. Many are into asking forgiveness but not confessing. We confess; God forgives.

This is a good time to talk about same-sex accountability groups. More people in the culture are ready to be accountable to others and to be held accountable.

Study 9. Nehemiah 9—10. Confession & Commitment.

Purpose: To understand that confession of our sins leads us back into a commitment of a renewal of the covenant relationship we have with God.

Question 1. It seems strange to us that our family's sins would be brought out into the open so clearly. However, these returning exiles are very aware that the last one hundred years or more in exile are a result of turning away from God and his covenant. And they don't want to make the same mistakes their forefathers made.

Question 2. Confession is agreeing with what God says and knows about us. Breaking God's laws and falling short of his standards for us is serious business. Our starting point is to own up to this lack in our lives; this is confession. There is no real renewal or recommitment to God without confession.

Question 3. We are not in the family we are in by chance. God knew which family to put us in. If you are a Christian and other family members are not, God wants to use you in reaching them. Your familiarity with your family history is important to your understanding and reaching them with the good news of Jesus Christ.

Question 4. Do you know who the Christians of your family heritage are and what they did for the Lord or things they learned in serving the Lord? The danger here is twofold. We feel the hurt of the sins of our family against us, so we cannot get a very good perspective on thinking about helping them. Second, we get into a stage of denial and do not face our family history honestly. In the first case we deny any good or positive things in our family. In the second we do not take any responsibility for our family and its history. God can bring healing into our families through us. But it will mean that we will have to rise above the hurt we feel and gain a perspective on how God feels about our family members.

Question 5. Israel knew they had experienced the judgment of God because of the unfaithfulness of their forefathers. If character traits and tendencies are passed down from one generation to another, we should learn from their mistakes if we don't want to repeat the sins of the past.

Question 6. What chance would the common people have to make it in Jerusalem with God if the leadership is not committed and ready to lead the way?

Question 7. It would be hard to think of any group of people not included in these lists. If all the leadership and most of the people in any religious group are not behind the covenant (commitment), there is not much of a chance it will be accomplished.

Question 8. There is a lot of serious commitment here. Are we prone to be this serious about our covenants with the Lord, such as Bible study, prayer, fellowship and witnessing?

Question 10. It is hard to fulfill your spiritual responsibilities to God when you are not doing the mundane things like Bible study, prayer, fellowship, witnessing, tithing, giving to the poor and so on. If we cannot abide by God's rules, we will probably not be too creative in worship, praise and adoration of the Lord.

Question 11. Because the returning exiles are so few, unless all are serious about helping out they will not become a functioning nation again. It will take sacrifice and work on everyone's part to make life happen as it should in Jerusalem.

Study 10. Nehemiah 11. Big Decisions.

Purpose: To broaden our thinking about where we live and work, making decisions in light of God's purposes rather than in light of our materialistic reasons.

Questions 1-3. Note that the leaders of the Jews did live in Jerusalem. The seat of government was in Jerusalem. Some people chose to live in Jerusalem. Certain people's jobs precluded that they live in Jerusalem, and the rest of the people who were needed in the city were chosen by lot. Remember, every family (except priests) owned land. If they lived in Jerusalem they either traveled out to till their land or had others farm it and share the produce. The land always belonged to the family. It could be sold, but it returned to its original owner at least by the year of Jubilee. In an agrarian society most people make their living by tilling the land. Craftsmen developed, and we have already seen that in the listing of the people who built the wall. Many craftsmen still had family land that was tilled, either by other family members or by sharecroppers. Most of the variety of jobs was needed to keep the temple and religious worship going.

Questions 4-5. Since the temple is in Jerusalem, it is imperative that a certain number of priests, Levites and temple servants live in Jerusalem for the ongoing functioning of the temple and religious worship (for example, when the gatekeepers are on duty they have to live in or near Jerusalem). Before the exile, Benjamin and Judah made up the southern kingdom usually referred to as Judah. If Israel's government was going to function properly, they had to have positions in the capital city filled. Remember, Jerusalem had not functioned this way for over one hundred years!

Question 6. Remember that the people were to give their tithes and offerings to the Levites, who collected them and put them in storehouses in Jerusalem. The Levites tithed this produce and gave it to the priests for their living. Probably other temple servants benefited from the tithes and offerings as well.

Question 7. If Jerusalem doesn't function properly as the government, all the Jews in Judah and Benjamin will be less safe and secure. In war the outlying towns would come into the walls of Jerusalem for safety and security.

Questions 8-10. This chapter implies that most people wanted to live on their land and not in Jerusalem. It is easy to see why this was so: for earning their living. Produce and things you make on your own land are not the means of barter today. There were some craftsmen in Israel at this time, but most income came from farming. Today little of our gross national product comes from farming, and that small percentage comes from very few people who farm. In this sense we are much more mobile in our culture. We could be moved by God almost anywhere to be involved in his kingdom building. God's kingdom is not a small piece of land anymore; it is the world. Acts tells us that God sent persecution to the Christians to drive them out of Jerusalem and carry the message to the whole world.

Now or later. Paul sees the church as the "true Israel." God's kingdom is not a place or piece of land, but it is in the hearts of every Christian. Jews became so attached to their land and their culture that Jesus had some very hard things to say to them and especially to the religious leaders of his day.

Study 11. Nehemiah 12. Service & Integrity.
Purpose: To see that all work is important to the building of God's kingdom. It takes many jobs to build the church, and we should not make strong differentiation between those jobs; contributing to the whole is more important than independence.

Questions 1-2. These jobs concentrate on what was needed to make Jerusalem, the temple and the religious practices function well. It takes many people to make it all work. The church operates the same way. We notice the music leader, but the person who is taking care of the toddlers in the nursery is just as needed for a properly functioning service.

Questions 4-5. It is important to recognize gifts within the body of Christ. It seems reasonable to believe that God gifts people in the body so that individuals and the church recognize the gifts and utilize them for the good of all. We should never downplay the gifts of helps and service while favoring the gift of leadership. If we do, we don't have a proper view of the church. All gifts must work together for the good of the whole.

Questions 6-7. God enabled them to build the wall, there was a renewal of the Word of God, and they all had a part in making the whole thing work. They had not had a religious identity like this for many years, and there was reason for much rejoicing. They felt God's presence and help, and it was obvious even to the people around Jerusalem that God was working for Israel.

Question 9. When we are experiencing unity and vision, Christians are prone to give gladly, but when there is little vision and unity, people give grudgingly. Note verse 44: they were pleased with the services of the priests and Levites, and tithes came in easily. When people do not give freely, the work of God struggles forward. We must also realize from verse 44 that it is God who commands us to bring our tithes and offerings, and to not do it begins to erode the vision and unity the body needs to move forward.

Questions 10-11. The bottom line is that if God's people do not support the ministries that are going on, they will come to a standstill. In Nehemiah's time, God was trying to get the people to bring their tithes and offerings into his storehouses so that the ministry would not be hindered. This was probably one of the few times that the collections were going well. At most times in Israel's history, the Levites and priests had to work their own land in order to make a living. If you have leaders in your group, you may want to ask how you can offer encouragement and support to them.

Now or later. Some of the needed jobs in your fellowship may not be so noticeable by others, but if the three-year-olds don't have a teacher or a good program, the parents of those children will lose interest in coming to your group.

Study 12. Nehemiah 13. Love That Challenges.

Purpose: To see how quickly we sinners can lose the ground gained by renewal and repentance, and to learn how to deal with sin boldly and quickly before it completely erodes the work of God in the body of Christ.

Questions 1-3. Even if it has been several years since Nehemiah's last visit to Jerusalem, it makes discouraging reading to see how quickly the leadership could deteriorate because of alliances with the people around Jerusalem. These petty potentates were not militarily strong enough to overcome Israel, but through their family intrigues, they had effectively neutralized Israel in its worship and commitment to God.

Question 4-5. Israel was easily moved to enthusiasm. The building of the wall did it for a while. We would have to say that their networking among the people of the land was also something that intrigued them and redirected their energies away from God. The nobles were constantly trying to better themselves with marriages to important people. This is the problem of mixing kingdom values with the world's values. The world's values have a way of eating up the kingdom values. Israel lives with heathen all around them and has for a long time. Their own religion is watered down by constant seeking to adapt to the culture around them.

Question 6. Nehemiah represents a single-minded person. Following God and keeping the faith pure are very important for Nehemiah. That purity is not something to be tinkered with. To lose it is to lose that relationship with God that enables you to keep moving forward with God. On the other hand, the people of Israel will let expediency determine what they will do and how they will act. When the leaders of a group do this, there is not much to keep the members from doing it.

Questions 7-9. One could wish that the text gave us more indication of what Nehemiah does to the high priest Eliashib. It is obvious what Nehemiah thinks about Eliashib because he drives his son out of his presence! Verse 25 needs to be understood in light of all that Nehemiah has poured into this project. He could easily see it all go down the drain if he does not take drastic action. Note that Nehemiah resorts to action and not to theory about the rightness or wrongness of what the people are doing. After his action he sets up people that he can trust to continue that action. He also recounts the history that should show them that this is exactly what caused Israel's downfall before. He is talking to people who have experienced downfall and misery because of their father's sins, and now they are repeating them.

Question 10. Within the body of Christ, when we fail to go to a brother or sister and encourage them back into obedience to God, we are partaking of the deterioration of our fellowship. We cannot sit on the sidelines and say, "Have you heard about so-and-so? Isn't it too bad that they are not walking with the Lord?" Nehemiah has the biblical perspective clear. He uses his leadership abilities to try and get people back into relationship with the Lord. If we were doing the same, we would not be ashamed to say, "Remember me with favor, O my God."

Don Fields is a divisional director with InterVarsity Christian Fellowship. He and his wife, JoAnne, live in Indianapolis, Indiana.

What Should We Study Next?

A good place to continue your study of Scripture would be with a book study. Many groups begin with a Gospel such as *Mark* (20 studies by Jim Hoover) or *John* (26 studies by Douglas Connelly). These guides are divided into two parts so that if twenty or twenty-six weeks seems like too much to do at once, the group can feel free to do half and take a break with another topic. Later you might want to come back to it. You might prefer to try a shorter letter. *Philippians* (9 studies by Donald Baker), *Ephesians* (11 studies by Andrew T. and Phyllis J. Le Peau) and *1 & 2 Timothy and Titus* (11 studies by Pete Sommer) are good options. If you want to vary your reading with an Old Testament book, consider *Ecclesiastes* (12 studies by Bill and Teresa Syrios) for a challenging and exciting study.

There are a number of interesting topical LifeGuide studies as well. Here are some options for filling three or four quarters of a year:

Basic Discipleship
Christian Beliefs, 12 studies by Stephen D. Eyre
Christian Character, 12 studies by Andrea Sterk & Peter Scazzero
Christian Disciplines, 12 studies by Andrea Sterk & Peter Scazzero
Evangelism, 12 studies by Rebecca Pippert & Ruth Siemens

Building Community
Fruit of the Spirit, 9 studies by Hazel Offner
Spiritual Gifts, 12 studies by Charles & Anne Hummel
Christian Community, 10 studies by Rob Suggs

Character Studies
David, 12 studies by Jack Kuhatschek
New Testament Characters, 12 studies by Carolyn Nystrom
Old Testament Characters, 12 studies by Peter Scazzero
Women of the Old Testament, 12 studies by Gladys Hunt

The Trinity
Meeting God, 12 studies by J. I. Packer
Meeting Jesus, 13 studies by Leighton Ford
Meeting the Spirit, 12 studies by Douglas Connelly